### ADVANCE PRAISE FOR Breaking Free: A Children's Book for Adults

"This book is the equivalent of a big, comforting bear hug for the soul. I want to just nestle into it and let it awaken what is known but too often forgotten in our do! do! do! world. An adult book for the frightened child in all of us."
Danielle Poirier, Producer "The Magnificent 16"

"Love the book! Easy read, simplifies a very simple concept that most people complicate. Brilliant expression of a process for reaching our fullest potential."

Ann-Marie Church, RMT

"I would recommend this book as a must read for anyone of any age. I love the way wise quotes are incorporated in each chapter and the clear chapter content. For a long time I have hoped to have a book to recommend to those doing high stress work in suicidology that incorporates the skills for coping with crisis situations. At long last I now have it!"

Frank R. Campbell, Ph.D., LCSW, C.T., Senior Consultant
for Campbell and Associates Consulting, LLC

"This book covers in relatively simple language the complex issues of making changes in life, learning to appreciate yourself and life in general. The image of the chick breaking free from the shell is a vivid one leading to an exciting sense that much of life is a letting go (breaking free) of attachments to thoughts that keep us from living to our potential. The quotes provide an opportunity for reflection."

Irene A. Brannan, M. A. (Psych), Spiritual Director

"This book took me by surprise. It's full of wonderful common sense, insightful observations and advice about real problems and real life."
Jens Petersen, Editor

"What a delightful romp through the woods of our lives – an invitation to smell the earth as well as the roses!This book is full of open-hearted encouragement, simple, clear wisdom and the warmth that only a good friend walking at our side provides."

Henri McKinnon, Director of Insight Counselling and Training

# Breaking Free

## A Children's Book for Adults

by Arlene Kawchuk and
Shirley Winlaw-Tierney, PhD.

To:
Jessica
With love,
Arlene
xoxo

To Jessica –
Love Grandma & Grandpa
Christmas 2013

Printed and bound in Canada
Second Printing December 2013
ISBN 978-0-9881300-0-5

Inquiries:
The Book Chicks
PO Box 81024
755 Lake Bonavista Drive SE
Calgary, AB
T2J 0N2

www.TheBookChicks.com

# Acknowledgements

Wesley Grunow—for his creative graphic skills displayed on the book cover

Jens Petersen—for his skilful editing of the entire document and his helpful suggestions

Layne Bauer for his professional photos that make us look chic.

Steven Ushioda for shepherding us through formatting with Scribe Inc.

# Table of Contents

# Introduction

Age does not necessarily bring wisdom, but it does bring a greater need for reflection. You know—looking back over your life and smiling at gentle memories, cringing at embarrassing moments, sighing over choices not made, grieving for all the losses, and ever wondering just how your life could have been different, better even.

We, the authors, have reached that age of reflection and have chosen to share, very briefly, what we have learned that helps our lives now to play out more closely in alignment with our dreams and goals.

The bookstores and libraries are full of self-help books. Many of them are very informative and offer good suggestions for living a healthier and happier life. In fact, a short list of our top favourites is included at the back of this book.

However, we see room for a short, fun book that offers a quick reminder of a dozen key points to living your own life fully, starting today. Meander along with our chick, Shelly, as she learns to break free of not only her shell, but also imagined restrictions; or read the adult content of the chapters; or ponder the brilliant quotations at the end of each chapter from well-known people, both historic and current.

Here are the underlying themes of this book:

Today is a new beginning of your life.

Let go of the past.

Start your engines.

Break free!!!

## Chapter One

# Life (Eggsistence)

*Shelly, the most important thing to know is that you were put here on earth to enjoy yourself, to grow, to learn, and to share your love with others.*

*On your mark, get set . . . GO! No more shell—just you, Shelly. Now you can explore that amazing path called LIFE.*

Life can be an amazing journey full of beautiful moments. Opportunities are abundant for finding joy, love, serenity, learning, laughter, and excitement. In fact, whatever you want is available for you to discover, and to incorporate into your life.

Unfortunately though, you may get caught up in an existence where you keep thinking that your life is still waiting to happen—when you graduate from school, or get that promotion, or when you get married, or the kids grow up, or when you retire. The fallacy in these scenarios is the belief that your life will get better in the future only when circumstances change.

But it's not events that change your life; it's how you respond to the events that makes a difference. It seems to be human nature to look outside of yourself to find your life, when you really need to be looking inward.

Are you living with energy and joy? Do you awake in the morning with a smile? Do you give thanks for your blessings at the end of the day? Answering yes to these questions indicates you are living and not merely existing. Answering no indicates you need to ask yourself what it would take for your life to become a beautiful journey.

You are currently living in that gift of time between your birth and your death. As that time passes, it becomes increasingly important that you take stock. Do not waste any more time. Only you can make your life better. When you hear yourself complaining, stop and ask yourself what you could do differently—or how you could make yourself feel different. Determine what kind of person you need to be and what you have to do in order to get the life you want. Devote some time to listening carefully to your inner voice.

Remind yourself: "This is my life, and I get to create whatever experience I want." Then smile, belly laugh, and hug someone. Be committed to bringing conscious energy into your life and to living in the present—right now.

Make changes.

Record dreams.

Create goals.

Spend time with friends.

Be open to opportunities, and

Read the rest of the chapters!

You are the only one who can give your life meaning, so if you're looking for it, start looking there—at yourself. Everything that happens to you will mean what you make it mean. It's up to you.

*Linda Richman*

• • • • • • • • • • • • • • • • • •

Live all you can; it's a mistake not to. It doesn't matter what you do in particular, so long as you have your life. If you haven't had that, what have you had?

*Henry James (1843–1916)*

• • • • • • • • • • • • • • • • • •

The first step to getting the things you want out of life is this: Decide what you want.

*Ben Stein*

## Chapter Two:

# Change
# (Eggstend Yourself)

*Change is a good thing. It can present itself as excitement or fear. Shelly, venture into the unknown with an attitude of excitement. Your fenced home has a gate. Open it slowly and go see . . .*

Occasionally it's good to check in with yourself and get a reading on how you are doing. Are you comfortable in your life? Do you have a routine and know what to expect?

That can be good. Routine often brings feelings of security and reduced stress. But it can also bring boredom and restlessness.

Usually what holds you back is fear—fear of the unknown. Yet it's that very unknown that could bring you a new spark of energy and passion and excitement. Venturing out of your comfort zone is often exactly what you need in order to banish that boredom and reduce that restlessness.

Sometimes change is forced upon you by external sources. When you look around, you see that not much stands still in this world. One major example is the astounding technological growth in the last century. Most of you have experienced the challenges of learning new techniques and methods generated by this growth. (Remember when the Internet didn't exist?)

Change can push you into discovering new abilities that you didn't know you had or send you journeying down a path that you didn't know existed. Change, whether it be externally induced or internally chosen, creates the opportunity for you to live more fully.

The time to create change is now. Start with small changes. Add an activity of choice to your life—especially one that helps you to slow down and touch your inner world. Take up yoga, or martial arts, or painting, or fly-fishing.

If you wait for a more appropriate time in your life, that time may never come. Expecting your life to change by itself is unrealistic. If you continue to do what you have always done, then you will continue to get the same results. So be a little bit daring and put yourself out there.

Look for change.

Create change.

Embrace change.

You are where you are because you want to be. If you want to be somewhere else, you have to change.

*Mark Victor Hansen*

• • • • • • • • • • • • • • • • • •

Only I can change my life. No one can do it for me.

*Carol Burnett*

• • • • • • • • • • • • • • • • • •

Change your thought and you change your world.

*Norman Vincent Peale (1898–1993)*

## Chapter Three:

# Mistakes (Ineggsact)

*So everything doesn't always land sunny side up—so what? Shelly, fluff up and shake out all your fears and faux pas—all your bloopers. Brush out and brush up. You are a very resilient creature, whether big or small.*

Now tell the truth—do you live your life in fear of making a mistake? You worry about what people will think of you. You berate yourself about your stupidity and beat up on yourself because you aren't perfect.

Well, here is some good news. There are only four kinds of mistakes that you can make. The first are the little everyday ones. The second are the bigger ones that have major consequences. The third are the mistakes made while trying something new. The fourth are not really mistakes, but rather outcomes over which you have no control.

Most mistakes are the little ones that are not important and that everyone makes. Perhaps you forgot to pick up milk on the way home, or you deleted an email message before you read it, or you locked your keys in the car. Either forget these mistakes or turn them into funny stories to share with your friends.

The bigger mistakes have consequences that are not so easily forgotten. You might leave the door to your home unlocked, and someone steals your valuable possessions. You might be driving when your foot slips off the brake causing a serious accident. The consequences from bigger mistakes, such as these, are heavily laden with emotion. Shock, guilt, and anger are very common. Eventually, though, you need to let go.

Here is where attitude makes a big difference. How you perceive or view things relates directly to how you think and feel about yourself. Mistakes are not the end of the world. They are a part of being human and a part of learning. They give you another lesson in accepting yourself as being less than perfect, but perfectly all right.

The third type of mistake can occur when you attempt something new. To find out if a new idea is workable, you have to try it. Poor results do happen. There are many famous people who have reported that they made innumerable mistakes before achieving their goal. The Wright Brothers spent years trying to get a plane off the ground. Thomas Edison took out a thousand patents before finding success.

The fourth type of mistake is not a true mistake. It is an unfortunate result of a good decision. Perhaps you quit your job, and the next one is worse. Perhaps you marry someone who turns abusive. Perhaps you invest in some stocks and the value drops.

The key here is to accept that you made the best decision you could at the time. Hindsight has always been more accurate than foresight. As long as you make decisions with the best of intentions, using the best information you have at the time, then you have done the best you can do, and it is time to move on.

In fact, the phrase, "it's time to move on," works for all four kinds of mistakes.

Let go of the past.

Look to the future.

Live today.

Freedom is not worth having if it does not include the freedom to make mistakes.

*Mahatma Gandhi (1869–1948)*

• • • • • • • • • • • • • • • • • •

Mistakes are a part of being human. Appreciate your mistakes for what they are: precious life lessons that can only be learned the hard way. Unless it's a fatal mistake, which, at least, others can learn from.

*Al Franken,* Oh, The Things I Know!

• • • • • • • • • • • • • • • • • •

Mistakes are the portals of discovery.

*James Joyce (1882–1941)*

# Chapter Four:

# Self-Confidence
# (Be a Bombshell)

*What a difference a day makes! Put on your "here I come world" attitude and march to the drum roll in your heart. Hesitations mess up the rhythm. Only you can hear your heart beating, Shelly.*

How often do you find yourself admiring those who seem confident in themselves, so sure? People who appear confident seem to be so comfortable with themselves, so self-aware, so alert, so knowledgeable, so upbeat, so in tune with those around them, and so not fearful of others' opinions.

Perhaps it is that last observation that is the most important factor. Imagine not worrying about what other people think, or more accurately, what you perceive that other people think. When you were little, you did what you were told, and you didn't do what you were told. Right from the beginning, you felt that tug between pleasing others and doing your own thing. Sadly, they just weren't always the same. To be independent, you sometimes had to displease, worry, or anger others.

Not much changes with adulthood. The pull to fit in and be accepted resists that push to just be yourself. It is not an easy task to find the balance between being real and still being perceived as normal.

Self-confidence is not taught in the school system and usually not at home either. Here are some tips to gain a little more of it.

Physically you need to have good posture—shoulders back and down, stomach in, chin up, and look ahead, not down. Check yourself in a mirror. Work on your posture. Make faces at yourself. Laugh. Now you are relaxed. Oh, and put a smile on your face.

Mentally focus on the areas in which you do well, such as gardening, golfing, caring for children, or balancing financial accounts. Emotionally take a temperature check—put negative feelings on the back burner to be attended to later, and count your good fortune in the moment. Then, and this is very important, focus on others and not yourself.

Putting on the outward appearance of self-confidence takes constant practice. After a while, just by looking confident, you will begin to feel confident. Others will reinforce that by treating you as a confident person.

When you feel good about yourself, you find yourself comfortable with others and don't stand out in any way. When you don't feel good about yourself, you believe that everyone is paying attention to you. Somehow feeling self-conscious creates a belief that people have nothing better to do than look at you, talk about you, and laugh at you. So when you feel self-confident, you are not in the spotlight. Yet when you feel self-conscious, you believe that you are in the spotlight. Strange, isn't it?

One of the bigger issues that prevents one from having self-confidence is comparing oneself to others. That person is more attractive. This person is smarter. This person is richer. This person is more talented. The list goes on and on. One of the most destructive things you can do to yourself is to make comparisons. You are judging from the outside how fortunate others appear to be. But you do not know how anyone else feels inside, and that is truly the most important factor.

The true beauty of self-confidence is the feeling of well-being, which makes it much easier to meet people on an equal footing. You are neither superior nor inferior to anyone else. You are simply a human being.

Acknowledge your strengths.

Practice good posture.

Smile.

Focus on others.

Believe in yourself! Have faith in your abilities! Without a humble but reasonable confidence in your own powers, you cannot be successful or happy.

*Norman Vincent Peale (1893–1993)*

• • • • • • • • • • • • • • • • • •

Too many people overvalue what they are not and undervalue what they are.

*Malcolm S. Forbes (1919–1990)*

• • • • • • • • • • • • • • • • • •

Once we believe in ourselves, we can risk curiosity, wonder, spontaneous delight, or any experience that reveals the human spirit.

*E.E. Cummings (1894–1962)*

## Chapter Five:

# Creativity
# (Eggspress Yourself)

*You are a fertile, creative and inspired being. You can be a brown, yellow, or white chick, or you can be a chicken and hang back in the coop. Strut your stuff, girl! Look for that original swagger, Shelly.*

When you think of the word *creativity*, do you think of drawing, painting, acting, singing, playing a musical instrument, dancing, or some other art form? Absolutely. All of those activities are beautiful ways to express oneself creatively.

However, they are not the only means of creative expression. There are countless ways to express yourself, and it shows every time you do something just a bit different from the ordinary or the expected.

Examine various areas of your life and look for creativity within them. Your home is an example—how you organize your furniture, how you group paintings on a wall, the colours you choose to paint the walls, the decorations you choose to display—it is your own creative space.

Consider how you dress and how you style your hair. Every time you walk out the door you present a creative version of yourself. If you don't believe your presentation is creative, then make a change. Get your hair cut in another style. Buy a scarf and tie it in different ways. You can reinvent yourself again and again.

When you are building a wooden structure and the manual doesn't make any sense, you can throw it away and follow your instincts. The result won't look like the picture, but it will be yours. When you are following a recipe and you don't have some of the ingredients, then trust your intuition and make substitutions. The result will be your own concoction.

Create your own quilt of life. Use all the colours. Use all your senses. Express your dreams. Take a new class—art, baking, woodworking, writing. What begins in a class can become a creative beginning. Write down your thoughts. Keep a journal. Track your ideas. Dare to express yourself and be different.

It is so important to have dreams—and with dreams comes imagination. Do not put out the light of what you can see in your own vision. Dare to make it come true.

To create is to express.

Close your eyes.

Envision.

Embellish.

Find the match; turn on your light.

Creativity comes from trust. Trust your instincts. And never hope more than you work.

*Rita Mae Brown*

• • • • • • • • • • • • • • • • •

Imagination is the beginning of creation. You imagine what you desire, you will what you imagine, and at last you create what you will.

*George Bernard Shaw (1856–1950)*

• • • • • • • • • • • • • • • • •

Creativity requires the courage to let go of certainties.

*Erich Fromm (1900–1980)*

## Chapter Six:

# Talents
# (Ordinary Be Devilled)

*Every leader has her critics, Shelly. Please yourself, and you will please most others. Forget the couple of gossips clucking away in the corner. You are doing what you are good at, and that will be your success.*

Did you read the chapter title and think to yourself that this chapter didn't apply to you? Did you think to yourself that you don't have any talents? If that happened, you're wrong. According to the Cambridge Dictionary of American English (2007), a talent is "a special natural ability to do something well." Everyone has talents—including you. A mother has many talents, ranging from maintaining a household, to administering first aid, to being a chauffeur. A child has talents for feeling free and understanding how to have fun. An executive has talents for overseeing day-to-day operations while holding a clear vision for the company. Many people have a talent for making others feel warm and appreciated. The real problem may be that you do not recognize your own talents.

So many messages likely exist in your mind because you were taught them from an early age. One of those messages revolves around the concept of being humble and letting other people shine. You may have learned to praise others but not to praise yourself. Recognize that you are as important as others.

The whole concept of belittling yourself in order for others to appear better is a concept that is not valid. Belittling yourself has a negative effect on you as an individual as well as on the whole world. For if people hide their talents in order to put forth the notion that they are not at all special, then we live where talents are hidden and wasted.

There is a theory that people are not afraid to fail, but instead are afraid to be successful. But is it fear? Or is it that old message that says you are not supposed to be too good at anything because it might make others feel bad?

How silly is that? If you have a talent for bookkeeping, then you can help the many who do not share that talent. If you have a talent for organization, then you can be the leader, or the moderator, or the manager, while other people shine at the tasks that they do well.

So, the one downside to not using your talents is that the world is deprived of them. The other downside is the probable lack of self-esteem that envelops you. When you deny that you have talents, you are giving yourself the message that you are not good enough. Now stop and think about that. Your own self-talk puts you down. What a difference it would make if you were grateful for the gifts or talents that you have. Picture the world filled with depressed people who don't acknowledge their gifts. Picture the world filled with confident, happy people maximizing the use of their gifts. Which picture do you prefer?

There is a vast difference between bragging about yourself and just being you. It is not necessary to tell people how great you are. It is necessary to tell yourself how great you are—that you are worthwhile and that you can contribute to this world in which you live. Others may notice and give you compliments. They may acknowledge and appreciate your contributions. However, what is even more important is that you do your best and take pride in that. Feeling good about what you can do is another way of feeling good about you.

Be yourself.

Appreciate your talents.

Celebrate your success.

If you have a talent, use it in every which way possible. Don't hoard it. Don't dole it out like a miser. Spend it lavishly like a millionaire intent on going broke.

*Brendan Francis*

••••••••••••••••••

Work while you have the light. You are responsible for the talent that has been entrusted to you.

*Henri-Frederic Amiel (1821–1881)*

••••••••••••••••••

Hide not your talents, they for use were made. What's a sundial in the shade?

*Benjamin Franklin (1706–1790)*

# Chapter Seven:

# Opportunity
# (Crack It Open)

*Are you ready, Shelly? Don't hang back; get those chicken feet wet. While in the water, you may find a raft! But on shore, you would miss that golden opportunity.*

Have you ever wondered what opportunity looks like? Sometimes the word *opportunity* gets confused with another word called *luck*. However, there is a big difference between opportunity and luck.

Luck requires no effort—it just happens. Opportunity requires some effort. If you sit at home and wait for one, you are not likely to find it. Even though there is a familiar saying that "opportunity comes knocking at your door," it's just not that easy.

You need to open yourself to the prospect of seeing an opportunity that may give you a chance to realize your dream. In which case, you need to be clear about your goals. You need to be able to visualize what type of opportunity you are actually looking for.

Is it a job change? Take the time to think about how you would describe the perfect job. Then talk to everyone you know about what you want. Keep your ears and eyes open. Often the opportunity shows up where it is least expected. If you are looking for a life partner, reflect on what characteristics are important to you and let them be known. And perhaps most importantly, do not put your life on hold while waiting for an opportunity to happen. Continue to live your life fully and happily while staying alert for that opportunity.

It is much easier for an opportunity to find you if you move out of your normal comfort zone and place yourself where what you desire is more likely to appear. An opportunity to make new friends is not likely to happen in your own front room. But if you join a fitness club or a choir or a book club, or whatever interests you, you will meet new people who have an interest in common with you.

Another common way for opportunity to present itself is through a crisis. The loss of a job often precedes the finding of a better one. The devastation of a broken relationship often precedes finding a better mate after the healing process.

Is it coincidental that better jobs and better mates come along? No, there are reasons. First, it is critical to examine what went wrong with the last job or relationship. Second, it is necessary to figure out what would need to be different for the next one to be more successful for you. Third, it is crucial to let people know your needs and to put yourself out where opportunity is likely to exist.

Sometimes you may miss an opportunity because you were not paying attention, or you had a preconceived notion of what it would look like. Opportunities take no special shape, occur at no special time, nor in any particular place. So even though you may miss some of them, don't miss all of them!

Be open.

Analyze.

Visualize.

Put yourself out there.

Opportunity is missed by most people because it is dressed in overalls and looks like work.

*Thomas A. Edison (1847 −1931)*

• • • • • • • • • • • • • • • • • •

The Chinese use two brush strokes to write the word *crisis*. One brush stroke stands for danger; the other for opportunity. In a crisis, be aware of the danger but recognize the opportunity.

*Richard M. Nixon (1913−1994)*

• • • • • • • • • • • • • • • • • •

There is no security on this earth, there is only opportunity.

*General Douglas MacArthur*
*(1880−1964)*

## Chapter Eight:

# Listening
# (Tap, Tap, Tap)

*You are given two ears and one mouth. Guess why? It is so you can listen twice as much as you speak, Shelly.*

L istening is a skill that can be learned through practice. It doesn't come naturally. Most people take for granted that listening is very easy, yet what is the biggest issue raised when people don't get along? Yes, it's communication. By definition, communication consists of one person talking and one person listening. Too often, what happens is that while you are speaking, the other person is busy figuring out what to say next. Or worse, both of you are talking at the same time. Listening is not occurring at all.

In order to listen, you need to put your own thoughts on hold. Listening is an activity. It requires physical presence. It helps to face the person and have eye contact, to lean toward the other person with an open body position and to relax. Even on a telephone, physical presence is a positive aid to listening. Listening and talking while multi-tasking allows for basic messages to be passed back and forth, but does not allow for any in-depth communication.

Many disagreements arise because you don't understand what the other person is saying and *you* are not being understood. Naturally you try harder to get your point across and so does the other person. When you find yourself in such a situation, start listening and make sure that you understand what the other person is saying. Then tell the other person what you heard—get clarification to make sure you are clear. There is no implication here that you agree with the person, just that you are able to hear his/her point of view. Once someone knows that you are actually listening and understanding, that person is then able to listen to you. It is called taking turns.

Always be sure to ascertain if the other person wants you to engage in conversation. If the person asks you to listen because he/she really needs to talk, then you won't get a chance to talk. Another time, though, when you need someone just to listen to you, that person will be there for you. It's a different way of taking turns.

Remember that listening is not problem solving. According to Dr. John Grey in his book *Men are from Mars; Women are from Venus*, there is a greater tendency for men to want to leap straight to problem solving than for women. But both men and women can find themselves believing that they need to give advice. A good rule is to give advice only when you are asked to do so.

Remember too, that listening is not a time for making judgments. When someone reveals something that is meaningful, do not make little of it or scoff at it or make fun of it. The more you accept what you hear and the more you share, the closer you get to the other person. Listening means holding sacred what is given to you by another.

Listen.

Clarify.

Speak.

Courage is what it takes to stand up and speak; courage is also what it takes to sit down and listen.

*Sir Winston Churchill (1874–1965)*

• • • • • • • • • • • • • • • • • •

Years ago, I tried to top everything, but I don't anymore. I realized it was killing conversation— when you're always trying for a topper, you aren't really listening. It ruins communication.

*Groucho Marx (1890–1977)*

• • • • • • • • • • • • • • • • • •

It is the province of knowledge to speak, and it is the privilege of wisdom to listen.

*Oliver Wendell Holmes (1809–1894)*

# Chapter Nine:

# Friends (Alter-Eggos)

*Shelly, I'm here for you. I'll give you my hand and you give me yours. Let's share this journey of life—let's be friends.*

Friends are universal blessings. When you have friends, you are wealthy. With friends you can share your joys and sorrows and discoveries and thoughts and feelings. With friends you feel safe.

Yet many times people have confessed that they don't have any friends and don't know how to find any. The reason for their predicament is much like everything else in life worth having—it takes work, time, and energy. Friendship usually does not just happen. It builds over the course of time and demonstrates the ability to survive crises and heartbreak.

Friends are not always convenient, because in order to have a friend, you must first be a friend. In order to be a friend, you must be available for that person, to listen, to empathize, to care. Friends are special people who come into your life and offer a reciprocal arrangement— they are there for you and you are there for them, through the good and the bad times. There are many characteristics that define a friend. Dependability is a main one. A friend can be counted on to come over when asked and to offer help when needed. A friend is someone who cares so much about you that he/she will do whatever possible to enrich your life. With even one friend you are not alone.

A second characteristic of friendship is mutuality. Both people share their lives with each other. Sometimes you may call a person your friend, when, in fact, that person takes from you but does not give to you. Friendship must be a two-way street, except for those times when one is in need, and then friends take turns supporting each other.

A third characteristic of friendship is acceptance. A true friend accepts you just the way you are with no attempt to change you. A true friend does not judge you nor have expectations of you. A true friend is an automatic boost to your self-esteem.

It is not possible to have many friends, at least not of the caliber that is being discussed here. You have limits on your time and energy, and you must utilize them as best you can. Therefore, it is important to choose well and to know that the people you call friends are as worthy of you as you are of them.

One of the more common obstacles to having one or more friends is not being vulnerable enough to get to know someone else. It takes courage to open up to someone, while giving that person the time to open up to you. It also takes time because you need to develop enough trust to reveal yourself to another.

If you believe that no one wants to be your friend, then ask yourself if you want to be a friend. Are you willing to embrace the journey of getting to know another human being? Are you willing to invest not only your time but also yourself in the process?

Smile.

Lend a helping hand.

Share yourself.

The only way to have a friend is to be one.
*Ralph Waldo Emerson (1803–1882)*

••••••••••••••••••

Nobody sees a flower—really—it is so small
It takes time—we haven't time—and to see
Takes time, like to have a friend takes time.
*Georgia O'Keefe (1887–1986)*

••••••••••••••••••

A friend is one who walks in when the rest of
the world walks out.
*Walter Winchell (1897–1972)*

## Chapter Ten:

# Forgiveness (Eggsonerate)

*I forgive you, Shelly. What a powerful statement that is. Neither one of us is goof-proof. To forgive each other knocks down the hurt and resentment and leads to a better relationship—for us.*

*F*orgiveness is a word that can be confusing. It can sound as if you are being called upon to tell someone that whatever atrocious act has been committed was just fine. Only you may not feel that way—probably don't feel that way. Instead, you may feel outrage or resentment or hurt. Just what are you supposed to do with those feelings? You can't pretend that they don't exist. So accept how you feel and take time to vent. After you have given yourself time to wallow in those ugly feelings, stop and consider that forgiveness may be more for you, the person doing the forgiving, than it is for the one being forgiven.

In order to let go of painful past events, it is necessary to experience the emotions, move to a place of acceptance of what has happened, and then forgive those who have erred against you. When you stay angry or stay hurt, you use up precious energy that would be so much better used for positive thoughts and actions. That poisonous energy gets rekindled almost daily, as events or people or songs remind you of your grievance. Then you start thinking all over again about what happened. You are miserable.

The wound does not heal; it doesn't even grow a scab. The person who suffers continually is you; the perpetrator does not carry the wound.

By forgiving those who have wronged you, you release the poisonous energy that resides within you. You feel a huge weight lifted. Suddenly there is room for hope. You feel strong because now there is room for positive feelings after you have discarded the negative ones. There is freedom in forgiveness.

Forgiveness does not come quickly or easily for most people. Occasionally you may read or hear about a few rare people who immediately offer forgiveness to the drunk driver who killed their child, or to the person who killed a family member. How do they do that? Perhaps they have come to understand how truly self-defeating it is to harbour anger (and they likely are grounded in a faith of love).

You have much energy that is often untapped, yet there is still a limit to how much negative energy you can carry and still lead a happy life. Negative energy colours the whole world. Walking down a street and looking at strangers can give you a glimpse of those who are beaming positive energy, those who are exhausted, those who have settled for less than they

either want or deserve, and those who radiate negative energy.

What you carry within can be seen without. You
can't fool people for very long. Your words, your attitude, and your actions quickly betray how you really
feel about yourself. If you harbour bitterness and
rage, they will show up in your life and affect not
only you but also those around you. You owe it to
yourself and to your loved ones to release all negative energy, forgive those who have hurt you, and
move forward with your life.

Hurt.

Vent.

Let go.

Forgive.

The weak can never forgive. Forgiveness is the attribute of the strong.

*Mahatma Gandhi (1862–1948)*

• • • • • • • • • • • • • • • • • •

Life is an adventure in forgiveness.

*Norman Cousins (1915–1990)*

• • • • • • • • • • • • • • • • • •

The practice of forgiveness is our most important contribution to the healing of the world.

*Marianne Williamson*

## Chapter Eleven:

# Happiness (Eggsaltation)

*Can you do the chicken dance, Shelly? Or do you prefer to sit and watch? Joy is in the immediate moment. So at the very least, stand up and clap your wings. Happiness can be contagious, you know.*

"The pursuit of happiness" is an interesting right to have. Indeed, everyone is entitled to be happy. But what does it mean to pursue happiness? Those words can be confusing because it sounds as if happiness is out there somewhere and you have to go searching for it. You may buy into the false perception that something is going to do the trick. And so you wait and wait, knowing that it is right around the next corner.

You may believe that you have to diet and exercise, or improve your education, or get a job promotion with a larger salary, or start a family before you can find happiness. But have any of these in and of themselves ever been known to create instant happiness? You may turn to the self-help books, personal growth courses, travel, and prayer. All of these can be very helpful—what they point out is that happiness resides within and not without.

There are two different ways to travel through life. One way is to keep your eye on the destination—a bigger house, a better car, a new relationship, or a slimmer body—whatever your next goal happens to be. The other way to travel is to keep your eye on the journey itself—to be present in the moment. Experience the joy of playing with a puppy; experience the beauty of a sunrise; experience the accomplishment of a task—all of these can give you moments of happiness.

When you pile up moments, you end up with what you wanted—happiness. For happiness is a state of mind. How else do you explain those who have little wealth and are happy, or those who are disabled in some way and are happy, or those who have experienced great tragedy and are happy?

So what is the deciding factor? What is the formula to ensure happiness? Is there a formula? Well, possibly. In order to find happiness you have to be happy.

What? Does that sound foolish? Well, think about it. This whole book is about the chick hatching from the egg. No doubt you have heard the debate about which came first—the chicken or the egg? Well, why not a corollary for happiness? Which comes first—finding happiness or being happy?

Happiness, like so much of life, is dependent upon your self-esteem. It seems a safe bet that people who do not feel good about themselves do not feel happy. Conversely, those who know that just by being human, and therefore unique, they are special and can be happy.

Feeling worthy cannot be stressed too much. <u>No one can be you as perfectly as you can</u>. Believe it, trust it, and know that you deserve happiness.

Whatever is not working in your life—change it. Don't wait to be happy. On your journey to being the best you can be, enjoy your travels and feel happiness in the fact that you are alive and on this beautiful earth.

Be present.

Experience moments of joy.

Know you are special.

Happiness is a butterfly, which, when pursued is always beyond our grasp, but which if you will set down quietly, may alight upon you.

*Nathaniel Hawthorne (1804–1864)*

••••••••••••••••••

Happiness depends upon ourselves.

*Aristotle (344 BC–322 BC)*

••••••••••••••••••

All I can say about life is, Oh God, enjoy it!

*Bob Newhart*

## Chapter Twelve:

# Love (Fully Done— Handle with Care)

*There are dozens of ways to love and be loved. Wouldn't it be wonderful to experience all of them? Because, you know, Shelly, Love is all there really is.*

According to the Bible, there are three main ingredients for life—faith, hope, and charity, and the greatest of these is charity. The word *charity* has since been translated into the word *Love*.

*Love* is a word that has many different variations. You can love the sunrise; you can love kittens; you can love your neighbour; you can love your children; you can love your partner; you can love your job; you can love yourself; you can love the Divine Being. The one constant is that no matter what or whom you love, you feel joyously completed. The actual degree and form of love may vary, but everyone has the capacity to love much and to love often. There is no limit to the amount of love within you.

Typically when you speak of love, you are speaking of love for another person. But do not forget that the most important person to love is yourself. Some people say that they don't really understand love. Some say that they have not experienced being loved and therefore cannot love. But the beauty of love is that it is cyclical. When you love, you tend to create love. There is no question that it is beautiful to feel loved and to be in a situation where you and another person share a mutual love.

Love is an opening up of your heart, mind, and soul. It is giving without expectations. It is giving without fear of rejection. True love does not come with strings attached. There are false loves that can be really confusing. Know this: If the love is real, it does not depend upon what you do or who you are. Real love accepts, supports, and appreciates. If you are loved when you do the right thing, and not loved when you do the wrong thing, then you are not loved at all. You are the victim of manipulation.

You do not have to change yourself in order to be loved, but loving yourself is first and foremost. You can seek to be yourself and to be with those who like you just the way you are. You are lovable; you are worthwhile; you have value just because you are unique and human.

When you are able to accept yourself with your own mix of strengths and weaknesses, you become ready to acknowledge others who are also wonderful. To love yourself and others removes most of your self-doubt and your self-consciousness. You become able to live in the present in which the past is history and the future has yet to come. You become more alive and more involved and life takes on a beautiful glow.

Love and BREAK FREE!

One word frees us of all the weight
And pain of life: That word is *love*.

> *Sophocles (496 BC–406 BC)*

• • • • • • • • • • • • • • • • • •

Love is changing the world one heart at a time.

> *Thelma Box*

• • • • • • • • • • • • • • • • • •

To laugh often and love much . . . to appreciate
beauty, to find the best in others, to give one's
self—this is to have succeeded.

> *Ralph Waldo Emerson (1803–1864)*

# Bibliography

Albom, Mitch (1997). *Tuesdays with Morrie.* New York, NY: Doubleday.

Cordova, Kathy (2003). *Let Go: Let Miracles Happen*. Boston, MA: Conari Press.

Jeffers, Susan (1987). *Feel the Fear and Do It Anyway*. New York, NY: Ballantine Books.

LaRoche, Loretta (2001). *Life Is Not a Stress Rehearsal.* New York, NY: Broadway Books.

Mandino, Og (1983). *The Greatest Salesman in the World*. New York, NY: Bantam Books.

Radish, Kris (2002). *The Elegant Gathering of White Snows*. New York, NY: Bantam Dell.

Richman, Linda (2001). *I'd Rather Laugh*. New York, NY: Warner Books Inc.

Robbins, John and Mortifee, Ann (1997). *The Awakened Heart*. Tiburon, CA: H J Kramer.

Ruiz, Don Miguel (1997). *The Four Agreements*. San Rafael, CA: Amber-Allen Publishing.

Vanzant, Iyanla (1998). *One Day My Soul Just Opened Up*. New York, NY: Simon & Schuster.

Wilde, Stuart: (1987). *Life Was Never Meant to Be a Struggle*. Carlsbad, CA: Hay House, Inc.

# About the Authors

 **Arlene Kawchuk** has enjoyed careers in counselling and in the field of human rights, as well as studies in conflict resolution. As an author, her passion is creative writing, focusing on humour. Arlene lives in Calgary, Alberta, with her husband, Don.

 **Shirley Winlaw-Tierney** has enjoyed a full, satisfying, and exciting career life as a psychologist, teacher, trainer, public speaker, and manager. Currently she is involved with a program to foster spiritual living and is co-facilitating groups in grief recovery. Shirley lives in Calgary, Alberta, with her husband, Rob Hall.